See how plants grow
Fruit

Nicola Edwards

WAYLAND

Copyright © Wayland 2006
Editor: Penny Worms
Senior Design Manager: Rosamund Saunders
Designer: Elaine Wilkinson

Published in Great Britain in 2006 by Wayland,
an imprint of Hachette Children's Books

British Library Cataloguing in Publication Data
Edwards, Nicola
    Fruit. - (See how they grow)
    1. Fruit - Juvenile literature
    I. Title
    634

ISBN 10: 0 7502 4906 4
ISBN 13: 978 0 7502 4906 5

Printed in China
Wayland
An imprint of Hachette Children's Books
338 Euston Road, London NW1 3BH

The publishers would like to thank the following
for allowing us to reproduce their pictures in
this book:
Alamy: 14 (Darren Matthews). Corbis images:
cover and 4 (Jutta Klee). Ecoscene: 7 (Norman
Rout). Eye Ubiquitous: 11 (Gavin Wickham).
Garden Picture Library: 22 (Botanica). Getty
images: 6 (Peter Lilja), 8 (Michelle Quance), 13
(Michael Orton), 15 (Howard Rice), 16 (Dave
King), 17 (Johner), 18 (Martin Harvey), 19 (Hein
von Horsten), 20 (photos alyson), 21 (Richard
Nowitz), 23 (Key Sanders). Wayland Picture
Library: title page and 10, 5, 9, 12.

Contents

What are fruits?   4

Different kinds of fruits   6

Where do fruits grow?   8

Fruits around the world   10

Starting from a seed   12

The parts of a plant   14

From flower to fruit   16

How fruits spread seeds   18

How do we use fruits?   20

Grow your own fruit   22

Glossary   24

Index   24

What are fruits?

Fruits grow on flowering plants. They contain **seeds** which will grow into new plants. Fruits come in many different shapes, sizes and colours.

They may have smooth, shiny skins, thick peel or rough, hairy surfaces. They vary a lot in smell and taste.

▼ Many trees are flowering plants and produce fruits such as apples.

4

Fruits are important food for people around the world. They contain **vitamins**, which we need to stay healthy.

How many types of fruits can you see?

5

Different kinds of fruits

▲ Coconuts are the fruits
of the coconut palm tree.

You might think of
a fruit as something
you'd eat in a fruit salad,
such as a grape, melon or
mango. But a fruit is
something that contains
seeds, so there are many
things in nature that can
be described as fruits.

Fruit Fact

Not all fruits can be eaten.
In fact some are **poisonous**,
including many berries.

Fruits include things you might not have thought of, such as pea pods, tomatoes and aubergines.

▼ See the fruits growing on these aubergine plants.

Where do fruits grow?

If you walk around your local area, you'll see many different fruits, especially in summer and autumn when many fruits grow.

▶ These strawberries grow on a farm where visitors pick fruits fresh from the plant.

Some people grow fruits such as apples and pears on trees in their gardens, or plant beans, courgettes and peas. Others have greenhouses in which they grow fruits such as tomatoes and peppers that need warmer **conditions**.

▲ Workers on this farm in France grow apples to sell in many different countries.

9

Fruits around the world

Fruits grow all over the world, except in the areas near the North and South Poles where it is too cold. Many fruits such as papayas and bananas grow well in **tropical rainforests**, where it is very warm and wet. Other fruits, such as lychees, need plenty of rain.

▼ Oranges, lemons and limes are **citrus fruits**. Citrus fruits grow well in warm sunshine.

▶ These bananas are growing on a tree in a Caribbean rainforest.

Starting from a seed

Some fruits contain many seeds, others have just a few seeds and some surround a single large seed. Each seed is the start of a new plant. A seed has a hard outer casing. When the seed begins to grow, the casing splits open.

▼ Look inside these fruits. Some contain more seeds than others.

A green shoot is beginning to grow from this pea seed.

shoot

seed

The parts of a plant

The **roots** of a fruit plant spread through the soil, anchoring the plant in the ground. The roots take in water and **nutrients** from the soil. These travel via the **stem** to all the parts of the plant. The stem supports the leaves and flowers that develop from **buds**.

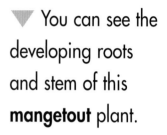

▼ You can see the developing roots and stem of this **mangetout** plant.

Fruit Fact

Some fruits, such as grapes, grow on climbing plants called **vines**.

Leaves make food for the growing plant. Flowers use their bright petals and strong scents to attract insects and other animals.

You can see the buds, leaves and flowers on this passion fruit plant.

15

From flower to fruit

The flowers of a plant produce **pollen**. When insects land on the flowers, they **fertilize** the plant by moving pollen from one part of the flower to another. The petals then fall and a fruit begins to form.

fruits

flower

Fruit Fact

Some fruits, such as pears and peaches, become softer and sweeter as they ripen.

▲ You can see the strawberries beginning to grow on this strawberry plant.

These blackberries change from green to red to black as they ripen.

How fruits spread seeds

Fruits help plants to spread their seeds so that the seeds will grow into new plants. Fruit plants spread their seeds in different ways – by air, by water or by animals such as birds and chimpanzees.

▼ This coconut floated on the sea until it reached land and began to sprout.

Sweet, juicy fruits encourage animals to eat them. The seeds pass unharmed through the animals' bodies and fall to the ground in their droppings.

▶ Seeds in this bird's droppings could sprout into new plants.

19

How do we use fruits?

We eat fruits such as apples, plums and apricots raw, or cook them in pies. Some fruits such as bananas and cranberries taste good when they are dried.

Fruit Fact

You can use lemon juice as invisible ink!

◀ Eating fruit is a good way to keep healthy.

Dried fruits such as **gourds** can be made into musical instruments. Fruits such as mangoes and papayas are used to make scented bath oils and shampoos.

▼ Pumpkins can be carved into shapes to make Halloween lanterns.

Grow your own fruit

Grow tomatoes from a packet of seeds. Fill a seed tray with soil. Plant a seed in each section and cover with a layer of soil. Water the soil to keep it moist. Tie a plastic bag over the tray and put it somewhere warm and light. When the seedlings appear, move them to a separate pot or put them in your garden.

▼ Follow the stages in your tomato plant's life.

Fruit Fact

When the tomato seeds start to grow, this is called **germination**.

How will you know when the fruits are ripe and ready to eat?

Glossary

buds
The parts of a plant inside which leaves and flowers develop.

carbon dioxide
A gas in the air that plants use to make food.

citrus fruits
Juicy fruits such as oranges, lemons and limes.

fertilize
When the male part of a flower merges with the female part so a fruit can form.

germination
The process by which a seed starts to develop into a plant.

gourds
A fruit similar to a pumpkin or a squash.

mangetout
A type of pea, but the pod is eaten too.

nutrients
Food in the soil which a plant sucks up by its roots to help it grow.

pollen
A yellow dust produced by the male parts of a plant. A seed begins to form when pollen fuses with the female part of a plant.

roots
The parts of a plant that hold it in the soil and suck up water and nutrients.

seeds
The parts of a plant from which new plants develop.

shoot
The beginnings of upward growth from a seed.

stem
The part of a plant that holds it upright.

tropical rainforests
Forests that grow in areas where it is hot and wet.

vitamins
Substances found in fruits that we need to keep us healthy.

Index

animals 15, 16, 18–19
buds 14–15
citrus fruits 10
conditions for growth 9, 10, 22
dried fruit 20
farm 8–9
fertilization 16

flowers 14–15, 16
food
    for fruit plants 14–15
    eating fruit 5, 6, 19, 20, 23
germination 22
growth 4, 7, 8–15, 16, 22–23

leaves 14–15
poisonous fruit 6
pollen 16
rainforests 10–11
ripen 16–17, 23
roots 14
seeds 4, 6, 12–13, 18–19, 22

shoot 13
stem 14
trees 4, 6, 9, 11
types of fruit 4–11
uses for fruit 20–21
vines 14
vitamins 5
water 14, 18, 22